dream jobs ™

I want to be a
CHEF

PowerKiDS
press

New York

Mary R. Dunn

Dedicated to my husband, Mike, a great chef

Published in 2009 by The Rosen Publishing Group, Inc.
29 East 21st Street, New York, NY 10010

First Edition

Editor: Amelie von Zumbusch
Book Design: Ginny Chu
Layout Design: Julio Gil
Photo Researcher: Jessica Gerweck

Photo Credits: Cover, pp. 1, 8, 10, 12, 14, 16, 20 © Getty Images; p. 4 Shutterstock.com; p. 6 © FilmMagic; p. 18 © AFP/Getty Images.

Library of Congress Cataloging-in-Publication Data

Dunn, Mary R.
  I want to be a chef / Mary R. Dunn. — 1st ed.
     p. cm. — (Dream jobs)
  Includes index.
  ISBN 978-1-4042-4471-9 (lib. binding)
  1. Cooks—Juvenile literature. 2. Cookery—Vocational guidance—Juvenile literature. I. Title.
  TX652.5.D86 2009
  641.5092—dc22

                                    2007051788

Manufactured in the United States of America

CPSIA Compliance Information: Batch #WR905080PK: For Further Information contact Rosen Publishing, New York, New York at 1-800-237-9932

Contents

Cooking can be lots of fun, but make sure to ask for an adult's help when you use knives or the stove.

4

Who's in the Kitchen?

The kitchen is a fun place to be. You can add **ingredients** to your favorite foods to create new dishes. You can get your hands messy rolling and patting **dough**. As you cook, wonderful smells fill the kitchen. However, the best part of cooking is tasting food you make!

Chefs are lucky because they get to work in a kitchen all the time. Most chefs work in **restaurants**, where they invent and prepare dishes to serve to **customers**. Chefs not only make food that tastes good, they also make sure that each plate looks like a work of art.

Chefs, like Jamie Oliver, sometimes go to farmers' markets to look for the freshest ingredients.

Food, Great Food!

To make great food, chefs must first pick out the right ingredients. Chefs make sure to buy the best meat and fish and the freshest **produce**. Chefs also find **spices** to season their dishes. Along with spices, chefs often use plants called herbs to season food.

Chefs can use the ingredients they buy to prepare dishes from around the world. For example, **pasta** is a well-liked Italian food. One way to cook it is with a spicy **sauce**. Sushi is a special Japanese dish. It is generally made with raw fish, **vinegar**, and rice.

Top chefs, like Emeril Lagasse, know that good pots and pans are an important part of making fine food.

A Chef's Job

In their kitchens, chefs keep busy with different jobs. Chefs spend part of their time putting together ingredients to make new **recipes**. At other times, chefs plan and cook specials, or the extra dishes that get added to the **menu** each day. Chefs have to guess what the hungry people coming to their restaurant will want to eat.

When chefs are not busy cooking food, they check their supplies to be sure they have all the ingredients they need. Many chefs also hire workers and give them jobs preparing and serving food at the restaurant.

Chef Mario Batali has starred in several TV cooking shows, such as *Iron Chef America* and *Molto Mario*.

Famous Chefs

Good chefs can become widely honored for the special dishes they make. Some **famous** chefs have their own TV shows on which they cook for a group of people. Those people get to taste some of the food while the chef tells funny stories.

Other well-known chefs write cookbooks. In these books, they share their secret ingredients. Sometimes, the chefs tell stories about the places where they worked and the important people they met. In his cookbook, *White House Chef*, chef Walter Scheib writes about cooking in the White House kitchen for two American presidents.

Rachael Ray generally teaches her readers and viewers how to make quick, easy recipes.

yum-o

Another well-known chef who has written cookbooks is Rachael Ray. One of her cookbooks is for kids. Ray likes to use new words to talk about food. For example, if food tastes great, you might say, "Yummy!" or "Oh, wow!" Ray put those two words together and made a new word, "Yum-o!"

Many members of Ray's family are cooks. As she grew up, Ray helped in their kitchens and learned about food. Her first job was selling candy in a store. Today, Ray has created many cookbooks, several TV shows, and a magazine about food.

These students are taking a cooking class at the Institute of Culinary Education, in New York City.

Chefs Go to School, Too

Most chefs do not learn all they need to know about cooking in their family's kitchen. Many people who want to be chefs go to culinary, or cooking, school. In some culinary school classes, chefs-to-be learn to plan menus. In other classes, students learn how to store, measure, and prepare different kinds of food.

Not all culinary classes are about food. Some classes teach students about safety rules and keeping a kitchen clean. Budgeting, or planning the amount of money needed to run a kitchen and pay helpers, is another important class.

As many famous chefs have, Gordon Ramsay started out as a line cook.

Team Workers

After culinary school, chefs may get jobs as line cooks at restaurants. Line cooks work at a station that makes one kind of food. Restaurants that serve seafood might have a line cook to prepare fish. In busy restaurants, there might be one line cook to make vegetables and another who makes only pasta dishes.

Chefs who work at a station where hot food is made are called hot-line cooks. At many restaurants, the head of the hot line is the sauté cook. This chef sautés food, or cooks it quickly at a high **temperature**.

Pastry chef Kikujiro Yoshida used 33 pounds (15 kg) of chocolate to make this dessert!

Sweet Chefs

Line chefs are important but so are pastry chefs. Pastry chefs make tasty breads and sweet **desserts**. Pastry chefs who work in large restaurants generally work in a room off the big kitchen where it is not so hot and busy. These chefs have to measure ingredients carefully and cook things at just the right temperature.

Many pastry chefs serve beautiful French pastries, such as open-faced pies called tartes and light, half-moon-shaped pastries called croissants. One fun part of being a pastry chef is getting to taste what you have made. Oo-la-la!

Thomas Keller is the chef and owner of the restaurants per se, in New York City and the French Laundry, in Yountville, California.

Working Their Way Up

Pastry chefs and line chefs spend many hours in the kitchen. They learn many skills there. In time, these chefs may become executive chefs. Executive chefs are chefs who are in charge of a kitchen. A chef must pass a special test to become an executive chef. Executive chefs generally run their kitchens with the help of a sous chef, or under chef.

The most accomplished chefs are master chefs. They have learned the highest culinary skills. To earn the right to be called a master chef, a chef must pass an eight-day cooking test.

So You Want to Be a Chef?

If you want to become a chef, start learning about food and cooking today. When you go to a restaurant, try different kinds of food. See what they look like and how they taste. Watch cooking shows on TV, too. If an adult is around, you can even use your kitchen to make up new recipes.

Share the food that you make with your friends and family. You can even tell them, *"Bon appétit!"* Chefs often use these French words to say, "Enjoy your meal!"

Glossary

customers (KUS-tuh-murz) People who buy goods or services.

desserts (dih-ZERTS) Sweet foods generally eaten at the end of a meal.

dough (DOH) Thick batter used to make some baked goods.

famous (FAY-mus) Very well-known.

ingredients (in-GREE-dee-unts) Parts.

menu (MEN-yoo) A list of food that is being served.

pasta (PAHS-tuh) A food made from dough and cooked in hot water.

produce (PRO-doos) Vegetables and fruits.

recipes (REH-suh-peez) Sets of directions for making something.

restaurants (RES-tuh-rahnts) Places where food is made and served.

sauce (SAHS) Something creamy that can be poured over foods.

spices (SPYS-ez) Seasonings from certain plants that are used to give taste to food.

temperature (TEM-pur-cher) How hot or cold something is.

vinegar (VIH-nih-ger) A sour liquid used in cooking.

Index

Web Sites

Due to the changing nature of Internet links, PowerKids Press has developed an online list of Web sites related to the subject of this book. This site is updated regularly. Please use this link to access the list:
www.powerkidslinks.com/djobs/chef/